Fierce Light

Linda Scheller

FUTURECYCLE PRESS

www.futurecycle.org

Library of Congress Control Number: 2017932591

Published by FutureCycle Press
Lexington, Kentucky, USA

ISBN 978-1-942371-25-0

For Andra and Rigel

Contents

IV. Glass Scepter

I.
What She Saw

Autoretrato Ultimo

Frida Kahlo (1907-1954)

I understand him and forgive him,
Even his dalliance with my sister.
He is a frog of exceptional ardor,
Moved to excess by women, their skin
In myriad hues, their flowery scent.
Life is a garden, and love a bouquet
We cannot help but breathe. He insists
I am his intellectual equal at least.
He tells everyone he is awed by my art
Since I interpret colors he cannot see.

He married me twice, and we live in
Two houses joined by a breezeway,
Mine *azul,* overlooking a courtyard
Filled with monkeys, deer, and little dogs.
My easel stands beside the bed where
I spend my days arguing with pain,
Limbs decaying, mad with misfortune.
I smoke and laugh at my own *chistes,*
Brush in hand, squinting at the mirror.

Drape the Communist flag over my casket,
Mi amor, when I die. Because I wish never
To return, bring my body to the crematorium.
Feed me to the furnace so my long black hair
Can burn, a writhing halo that flails goodbye.

Our Lady of the Chronicles

Murasaki Shikibu (c.973-c.1014)

*

An offering of
White chrysanthemums for you,
Translucent sister.

My brother's lessons
Taught me Chinese. Father sighed,
"Pity you're a girl."
*

*

Lake Biwa, widowed—
The full moon whispered to me
The Tale of Genji.

Lord Michinaga,
My patron, brought me to court
To teach his daughter.

Though he pursues me,
He slights my book, and therefore
Cannot have my love.
*

*

One courtesan's sleeves
Layered orange, green and mauve,
Presage her swift fall.

Clamorous cracked bell—
I wince, smile, and nod at some
Inelegant verse.

A drunken courtier
Mauls his concubine, roaring
At her frail protests.
*

*

Red amaryllis,
Wilting in the heat of court,
Longing for winter.

Secluded, writing,
Dawn's first light taunts me. I rise
To tend my Empress.
*

Toward Permanence

Julia Morgan (1872-1957)

Beauty is mathematical.
Nature's aesthetics—symmetry,
Pattern, geometry, inclination,
Variety of scale—these
Are nowhere else as evident
As here in California,
Eden at the edge of the world.
Mountains, dark forests,
Bright deserts, clouds,
The undulating Pacific,
Long valleys where
The mullion of a single oak
Punctuates a blue wash of sky—
For every region, I conceive
Elevations and textures to
Complement the natural,
Suitable to purpose.
Need informs design, but I
Consider the angle of light,
The climate, and the view.

As well as shelter, buildings
Should give pleasure—castle,
Cottage, gymnasium, or school.
Details embellish form.
Ironwork twins itself in shadow.
Polished wood holds depths
No paint can simulate.

Read the world's cities—
Styles and colors permutate
Our civilizations' virtues
And accomplishments.

Buildings should reminds us
Of our own potential strength
And the satisfaction of life
Committed to work,
Festooned in beauty.

Where Sovereign Music Leads

Barbara Strozzi (1619-1677)

Where sovereign music leads, to hill or vale,
In spirited delights that toss the heart
And join the souls of lovers, soon to part,
Or chambers of a king, with marble pale,
In graceful, wending dance that stills the gale
Of duty for an hour, holding quarte,
There must I follow in melodic art,
Composing music noble patrons hail.

But know my name will fade from lips and pen,
For men disdain my sex and only see
The fairest face and form as currency.
Despite the joy my songs engender when
Their notes reveal my rare ability,
Fame grants sweet immortality to men.

Observation

Rosalind Franklin (1920-1958)

The structure
   of discrimination
consists of
   twin strands,
disregard and
   ruthless tenacity
to hegemony.

It spirals,
   a drill,
boring holes
   into my
accomplishments, my
   honor, and
my health.

Rational insight,
   due recognition,
fall through,
   disappearing into
oblivion's vortex.

Flyology

Ada Lovelace (1815-1852)

Catalyst of scandal, my father, Lord Byron,
Fancied passion, like wine, as a temporary muse.
He married my mother, Princess of Parallelograms,
Who fled his profligacy when I was barely one.

I was thoroughly taught mathematics, inverse
Of his madness, and the Furies attended me,
Heedful of any impropriety. Divided by
Paralysis and crutches, my childhood
Was a cipher of headaches and bed rest.
I learned early that infirmity equals urgency.

The windows made visible the world of air
And its denizens, birds, whose flight suggests
Fairies, unseen but no less real. The gardener
Brought me a crow's wing, and my tutor
Provided me with books and a lap desk.
Proportion of wingspan to body length and
A frame durable yet light I discerned at twelve.
I theorized steam might someday hold me aloft.

Music is the daughter of logic and beauty,
Mathematics her lingua franca.
Verse is song reduced. Poetry, dance,
And my gilded harp spoke to me in clouds,
Positing new theorems, revealing
Patterns and causation, suggesting flight.

My *Notes* show how imagination
Penetrates the mysteries of nature.
Sequenced operations balance
Accuracy and speed. I predict that
Mortal minds will soon command
The agencies of constancy and change.

Six squared, my last year hovers over
Great Cumberland Place,
The ratio of life to time
Reduced to simplest terms.
Bright feathers of calculation,
Postulates and algorithms,
Flights of Bernoulli numbers
Dart across the engine of my brain,
This machine of nerves and blood
Fueled by poetry and numbers.

Metamorphosis

Maria Sibylla Merian (1647-1717)

God's Earth teems with multitudes, minute in size, prodigious in variety
And marvelous in transformation. Certain plants hide eggs as crèche
And feed emerging larvae, caterpillars, creeping now in close society
With predatory birds and wasps that lay their eggs in caterpillars' flesh.

The wasp eggs bring forth larvae that consume their host. Transformation
Fascinates me always. I seek, collect, and sketch new insects in captivity.
My book brims with larvae, pupae, imagoes, and eggs. Keen for exploration,
I traveled with my daughter overseas to Surinam, green cabinet of curiosity.

Collectors in Europe pay handsomely for specimens. One, the female toad
Of Surinam, keeps her eggs within her back until precocious offspring hatch.
She gropes for worms, star-fingered, on the river floor. Ninety days her load
Of larvae change beneath her skin. Emergent young and mother I would catch.

We sought and gathered wonders there. For my book's sake, this hierophant
Did nearly die of heat. Although my daughter ministered, we could not stay.
She helps engrave the copper plates, revealing metamorphoses in plants
That offer food and shelter. Nature proves time predator, and life its prey.

This etching shows a spider devouring a hummingbird its size. Strange
Creatures I have found and rendered. Patient still, I pray for full recovery
To print and sell my book, disclosing nature's interconnected change
In life-sized color plates, and thus to you extend the pleasures of discovery.

Viriditas

Hildegard von Bingen (1098-1179)

A valley opened between the eastern mountains, and the egg of the universe cracked. Out flew a hawk with three wings, alighting on a column of topaz. At a distance stood a column of wood, deeply carved with foxes vomiting gold. Between the columns rose a waxing moon, and I heard thunder and the voices of angels singing. Each note fell from the heavens and lay on the earth like dew. From these shining notes, green tendrils and bright leaves emerged, twining round the columns, climbing up and multiplying. The branches that encircled the topaz column blossomed with roses of every color, and the air was sweet with their fragrance, but the leaves on the carved wooden column withered and became a nest filled with serpents, rank with the stench of decay.

Then I saw a woman, dressed in robes of mist with emeralds in her hair, riding a white stag. Her path was a river of lilies. The stag halted and knelt beside the roses. She slid from its back and placed her hands over the animal's eyes. Rays of light issued from its antlers, and the column of serpents burst into flame. The woman spoke words in an unknown language, and the burning column became a waterfall filled with stars.

Singing

Georgia O'Keeffe (1887-1986)

Boneful note,
    measure of sand.
Dune, wind, sun,
      symphony.

Lightning strike, chasm,
    reaching snag,
      petal center,
        sky.

My nakedness, displayed,
    catapults over their heads.
My hands
    dance.

Violins.
Violet.
Violate.
Violzzz.

Skyscrapers loom,
    luminous.

Silence.

Sing, hands,
    sing.
Clutch.
Release.

Sing,
    flower, bone, shell.
Fingering.

Song.

Hill Top

Beatrix Potter (1866-1943)

Each crooked twig articulates the tree, a lace of bone
Achieves the body's architecture. These compel
My eyes to see, my hands to sketch and paint. I dwell
In nature's residence observing every detail, quite alone
With beauty and my animals. As fruit may hide a stone,
So grasses hide a teeming world of spiders and decay.
Soft busy mice, shrewd cats, the patient cold amphibians portray
The foibles of humanity in miniature. With line and tone,
I copy and experiment to render nature visible to all.
The picture letters blossomed into little books, which bought
My independence and my farm, my life among the sheep
And pigs within the realm of Wordsworth. Everything I sought,
I found in nature, learnt its lessons well, and heed its call
To flower in the shifts of light that cause the heart to leap.

Narcisse Noir

Anaïs Nin (1903-1977)

The club's darkness swallows me. Blind,
I touch the waves of my hair, smooth the silk
Of my dress over my breasts, my waist,
My thighs. Alain Romans grabbles the keys,
Seeking the floating straw on a burning sea.
I seek my father's smile in every lover,
His lessons in flesh the universal language
Of conquest through submission. Petite trapeze,
I learned young to swing wide on a ribbon of secrets.

A tablecloth floats, an eye in the face of the crowd.
Cigarette burns and purple rings pattern the fabric.
I see the aftermath of trysts, the seeds of deception.
I conjure bodies smoking, drinking, laughing,
Sweat dripping into open mouths. Narcisse Noir
Wafts up from my wrists and parts my own lips,
Forcing my gaze to linger on a dark-haired man
Who stares at me over his partner's shoulder.

Inhibitions drop like autumn leaves. Last night,
I stood at Henry's open window, naked,
My upraised hands on the wooden frame.
My body is freedom's currency. I am rich,
Heiress of incest and speculation.
Hugh is working, Henry is writing or fucking
Some tired whore, Allendy waits for me in vain.
I wander the streets, my purse a box of lies,
My face a mirror, my mind a volcano
Burning the cobblestones, raising new islands.

In Louveciennes, the mahogany desk awaits me.
Every flower of thought will be traced to its roots,
Every question examined with a fountain pen
The shade of my hunger, every passion recorded
In a journal covered with skin and filled with light.

II.
Reconnaissance

Red Emma

Emma Goldman (1869-1940)

When my nature led me to misbehave,
My father
Flew at me in rage,
Beating me until Helena
Succeeded in pulling him off.

Jewish girls,
He snarled,
Need only know how to make gefilte fish,
Cut noodles,
And bear their husband children.

He yanked from my hands
A French grammar
And threw it into the fire.

He planned my marriage.
I refused.
Helena and I left Russia
For America
And found all its promises,
Like Lorelei songs,
A ruse.

Whaea O, Te Motu

Whina Te Wake Cooper (1895-1994)

Before the *Pākehā* came to *Aotearoa,* we lived here. We have always been here, *tangata whenua,* our *tikanga* as old as the worlds. Men and women, children and chiefs worked together, growing crops and fishing, gathering seafood, hunting seals and moa, singing to the rising sun. This was our life before the *Pākehā* took the land. This was Māori land.

Though I am woman, *mana* is mine. Hear me. In the darkness of my birth, my father baptized me Joseph. My name changed, but not my heart. I listened to my father, the chief, converse with the elders and the Te Rārawa men speaking on the *marae.* I listened and grew strong. My digging became legend. Men of power asked for my opinion. I stand here to challenge the *Pākehā* and the Māori who say I should not speak.

Though I am woman, *ihi* is mine. Follow me. We march for Māori land from Te Hāpua to Parliament. Stop *Pākehā* land theft. Give us back the land.

Māori and *Pākehā* live in *Aotearoa* together. Let us work and pray together, men and women, children and chiefs, with love as our path.

Raised in the Harem

Huda Shaarawi (1879-1947)

Raised in the harem, married at thirteen,
I was owned and controlled by tradition.
Why do you perpetrate this slavery?
Seclusion degrades both men and women.

Remove the veil from your eyes.

Raised on the ladder of education,
I was taught by books and travel.
Why should we languish in ignorance?
Nescience degrades both men and women.

Remove the veil from your minds.

Raised by the cry for independence,
I was moved to assert my own being.
Why would I hide my face in shame?
Concealment degrades both men and women.

Remove the veil from your lives.

Aperture

Dorothea Lange (1895-1965)

I rambled into it. A journey
With my instincts to guide me,
A New Deal opportunity with Roy
Watching over us. The file grew
As the earth under people crumbled,
Heaving families from their homes
And shaking them off their farms.

The Resettlement Administration
Sent us out. It was hard but exciting.
Nobody told us what to do or how.
I was married with five children,
But I never quit. I looked for people
In trouble, first the Depression, later
The migrants, tenant farmers, evacuees.
I jotted down exactly what they said,
Photographed what I saw. I believe
It's important to really look around.
I can almost see what's happening
Behind my own head, 180 degrees.

I decided on photography when I was
Just a kid. Walking on Fifth Avenue,
I saw a display, went in, and got a job.
I learned how to develop negatives
From an old itinerant photographer.
He helped me put together a dark room
In the empty chicken coop. In a few years
I left home, went west. In San Francisco
I had my own business. Portrait photography.
But even so, I longed to do something else,
Something broader. Something important.

I began to photograph people in the streets.
Breadlines, demonstrations, transience, strikes.
Thousands of families streamed into California.
The government hired us to document the crisis.
I drove to the migrant camps and took my time.
To break the ice, I'd ask for directions, then
Talked about my life, told them everything
About my work, how the administration
Was aware of their troubles, interested,
Wanted the rest of the country to know.

I gave them all my attention.
Sitting in the dirt under an oak tree,
Drinking a cup of water in the shade,
Children would scoot in beside me
And poke at the lens, and of course,
I never said don't. Why would I?
The camera's part of my body.
A third eye. A second heart.
And what I saw in the camps,
In the fields, on the dusty roads
Ahead and behind me,
All around, was courage.

Culturist

Madam C. J. Walker (1867-1919)

Every woman has the right to look attractive as she defines it, following the styles of her time or modifying her appearance to suit her own tastes. Japanese women of the Heian Court removed their eyebrows and blackened their teeth. Do you call that natural?

Even back in my day, white women went to hair salons to get permanent waves. Fifty years later, they'd bake their bodies in machines and fry themselves on beaches in order to darken their skin. Those women weren't born with curly hair and brown limbs, but nobody chided them for changing what God gave them. No one took them to task for turning their backs on their ancestors or refusing to accept themselves.

White women are still paying good money and suffering pain to look more like us. What about these lip grafts and buttocks augmentations? It certainly seems to me there's a double standard here. Evidently, white women can alter themselves and appropriate the characteristics they envy in us with impunity, and yet we are criticized for abandoning our heritage when we culture our hair. Why is the privilege of altering what is natural granted to white women only? Blue hair, tattoos, body piercings, plugs, liposuction, fat transfers— as long as you're white, anything goes.

Our race is unjustly constrained if we are limited to what is deemed natural and expected to salvage some vestiges of pride only through self-acceptance. Unfortunately, there are still many who regard us as primitive or, at best, exotic. They prefer we stay simple and not question our designated place in society. It is gross injustice if a white woman can exercise the prerogatives of whim and transformation, but a woman of my race is supposed to passively accept herself and stay as she was born, effectively denying herself the right to choose her own identity.

Transformation is an American ideal. Rags to riches, that was my life. Orphaned at seven, a washerwoman for twenty years, I built a thriving business on beauty products and used my fortune for philanthropy. If I had stayed in my place, poor and powerless, I'd be stirring laundry 'til I died, but I wanted my daughter to go to school and live in a nice home. Acceptance is merely resignation. How you look, where you work, what you think—those are your choices.

If you don't like something, change it.

La Peregrina

Alma Reed (1889-1966)

Pixan-Halal, he called me,
Mayan for soul, grass by the lake.
Like Amalthea and Lucan,
Our two souls are one,
Eternally embracing.
Deprived of him,
I drifted like a cloud
Over continents and kingdoms,
Seeking magnificence in stone
And truth in art. I crawled
Over the bones of children
And walked beneath the ocean
On a path of white shells.
I searched for Hades
And found it twice,
Wandered the ruins of Carthage
Where Dido's curse still echoes
Against urns filled with brief lives
Offered up to Tanit, blood-thirsty
Goddess of the changing moon.

Sacrifice, loss, appeasement, silence.
I have fallen into wells so deep
Only lies could save me,
Placed rocks between gear wheels,
Carried messages into the light
With my own two bleeding hands.
Thrice beckoned the steps
Of Chichén Itzá, but only once
Can any woman climb
With beating heart inside her.

Forty years later,
It's hard not to think about
What we might have had
If he'd not been murdered
With his three brothers,
Standing by that moon-faced wall.
He sent me a Mayan ring,
And they say my photograph
Was in his hat when he waded
Into the Caribbean,
Trying to escape.

I am a little tired now, but
Tomorrow I'll feel better.
Call me after the operation.
I'll find some new story,
Some injustice, Atlantis,
Some deserving artist to promote.
I'll show those young journalists
What Alma Reed is made of.
Tonight though, I'll just lie here
And stare at the stars. Do you see
Those two? Those, right there?
Felipe's eyes. He waits for me.
He's watching me and waiting
For the dream from which
I never wish to waken.
It's been a long day.
I should sleep well tonight.

Folk Pornography Exposé

Ida B. Wells (1862-1931)

The mob says,
    lynching is justice.
The law says,
    all accused are innocent until proven guilty.

The white papers say,
    a Negro killed a white man and raped the white man's wife.
The colored press says,
    five days after the lynching, the wife confessed to her husband's murder.

The white sheriff says,
    there was no way he could stop the crowd from breaking into the jail.
The black witness says,
    the sheriff himself brought out the accused and handed him over to the mob.

The coroner says,
    the rapist was dragged to a clearing where a thousand men waited with
        guns, and after tying him to a tree, they made him strip, cut off his fingers
        and genitals, poked out his eyes, removed corkscrews of flesh, shot,
        and burned him.
The postcards say,
    slices of the rapist's liver were sold to children for a penny.

The legislators say,
    although they deplore these violent acts, lynching is a matter best left to
        the states.
The president says
    nothing.

You say,
    black men rape white women because colored women are immoral,
        lascivious, unattractive, and lack any control over their bestial nature
        or their men.

I say,

    white men have raped colored women for centuries, then lynch their own
        grandsons and call it honor.

Pieces of the Mosaic

Alice Paul (1885-1977)

If breaking windows brings the press, I will throw rocks.

We will picket the White House and starve in jail.
We will die unladylike deaths.

As you step down from your railroad car,
Contemplating your inauguration,
Wondering at the thin crowd,
We march on Pennsylvania Avenue,
Thousands of women from every state
Marching while onlookers spit and jeer.
As men strike us, policemen stand and watch.

I will use my gumption for the cause of equality.

Don't make me call you Kaiser.

The White Rose

Sophie Scholl (1921-1943)

We walked through darkness on narrow paths.
The meadow after woods was exultant with flowers.

Ja, Mutti, I remember Jesus.
So must you.

Wherever they burn books, they will also
In the end burn human beings, said Heine.

Our nation stands at the edge, silent.
The abyss writhes with endless shame.

Ach, Mutti, those few little years.

We bid the people resist, stop the murders,
End the war.

If speaking truth is treason,
Then our guilt is balefire.

Someone had to make a start.

The war is already lost, but
God's Scourge demands my head.

What does my death matter?

The leaflets fluttered like white birds
In the quiet atrium.

Murky black lake.
I dive,
Expecting to rise.

The sun still shines.

Barnstorming

Bessie Coleman (1892-1926)

I'm one of thirteen born to Texas sharecroppers.
Papa left when I was three. I walked four miles
To get to school, dust puffs rising from my feet,
And on that dust, I vowed to amount to something.

I followed my brother to Chicago and worked
As a manicurist in the White Sox Barber Shop
Where the pilots who'd flown in the Great War
Told their tales of dogfights and reconnaissance,
Fokkers popping from clouds, Dicta Boelcke
Maneuvers, scarves of smoke, spinning dives
And pulling up at the last second. I knew then
What I would be, but no one would teach me,
A woman who's colored. I had to learn French
And travel to Paris to earn my pilot's license.

I'll never forget the crash that killed Pierre,
The terrible shock of carnage, scattered flesh
That used to speak and kiss. That same day,
I willed myself to mount a plane and fly.
When I crashed last year, I thought of Pierre,
But I only broke one leg and a couple of ribs.

They've kept us down so long, it's only right
My people learn to fly. I aim to start a school
Teaching aviation to colored men and women.
Money comes from barnstorming. Queen Bess,
They call me. Thousands pay to watch me strut
All suited up in leather, climb into the Jenny,
Rumble down the runway, and lift up into blue,
The prop a busy blur and the engine throbbing.

Hammerheads, rolls and loops, spins and lines,
Skimming the crowd, all screaming and ducking
And clutching their heads. I laugh and ascend,
Wrapped in sky, leaning over the cockpit sill,
The land below patched green and brown,
And the crowd looking up, waving their tiny hats.

III.
Healing the World

The Miller's Daughter

Jane Addams (1860-1935)

I.

Before dawn, Chicago seethes
With bent figures gathering scraps.
Borrowed shoes and horse hooves
Slog through manure and cabbage.
The streets are lined with tenements
Crowded with shivering families
Whose four-year-olds sit squinting
Over basting, picking out threads
For pennies a day, coughing, while
In the factories, older siblings
Stand with aching arms and backs,
At toil before gnashing machines.
A girl screams, her fingers caught
And mangled. Another collapses.

The night whistle shrieks. The girls
Flock to dance halls, seeking husbands
But finding only misery in cheap whiskey
And brief pleasure. Their daughters
Take their place at the factory, and
Their sons play war in the alley.

II.

As a child, I watched my father
Stand at his millstone and lift a pinch,
Rubbing it between his forefinger
And flattened thumb, discerning
Flour from grain and grain from sand.
My own small thumb, soft with ease,
Discerned nothing, yet night after night,
I dreamed everyone in the world was dead

But me, in a blacksmith's shop, trying
To make a wheel without iron or fire,
Without knowing how. I searched
In sleep for sticks to whittle for spokes,
A log to shave into staves, and wondered
How one might bend without breaking,
How one might best strike a spark.

Family 21373

Tsuyako "Sox" Kitashima (1918-2006)

The wind sprays dust
   through the cracks,
     coating us
       on our cots.

My teeth grate
   against sand.

The child
   in the next room
     wails.

Too hot to sleep,
   I imagine the past.

The house in California,
   the land my parents
     were not allowed to own.

They truck farmed
   strawberries, lettuce, celery,
     tomatoes, and cauliflower.

After Japanese language school,
   my brothers and sisters and I
     joined them in the fields.

My sister and I plowed,
   one holding the reins,
     the other holding the plow.

Rainy evenings,
   I played piano.

My mother
    was always singing.

I remember *oshogatsu,*
    the men pounding rice,
        the women shaping *mochi.*

Perhaps that year,
    1941,
        someone forgot.

Perhaps
    someone swept.

Ministers and teachers
    disappeared.

Police shone spotlights
    through our kitchen window.

Radios and cameras
    were confiscated.

On telephone poles,
    notices appeared
        announcing the evacuation.

We could only take
    what we could carry
        with two hands.

We sold the tractor and the car,
    the furniture and piano
        for a pittance.

Our old horse
    that used to pull the plow
        was destroyed.

The bus took us
  to Tanforan.

We slept on hay
  in a horse stall
    heaped with manure.

For three months,
  we were incarcerated
    behind barbed wire.

Then soldiers holding guns
  took us by train
    to this concentration camp.

Don't go near the fence,
  the guards yell.

Mr. Wakasa
  walked too close.

He died,
  shot in the chest.

The wind shrieks.

I pull on my boots
  and tiptoe past
    my sleeping family.

At the toilets,
  a young mother stands in line
    with her daughter.

The girl clutches her doll,
  a *daruma* with one eye.

This eye is the girl's wish.

Our wish.

How long must we wait
    before she can draw
        the second eye?

Hear Ye

Maria W. Stewart (1803-1879)

Hear ye, for I have made myself a warrior
For the cause of those oppressed, a hissing.
Ye of fairer complexion, reproach us not.
Africa's sons and daughters yearn to rise
Above the condition of servitude. Methinks
Our merit deserves more than continual toil
At menial labor, excluded from the sciences
And vast reaches of knowledge. Prejudice
Cuts down our flowering youth, their perfume
Squandered and their beauty hidden. Had they
Education and the opportunity for progress,
Our daughters would rise from degradation
And aspire after leadership and affluence.
Had they equal opportunity to advancement,
Our sons would soon display their talents
In eminence and genius. Take pity upon us!
God has surely heard the prayers of Ethiopia,
Whose copious tears and lamentations
Stir in Him the promise of His vengeance.
The Lord has made the children of Africa
As intricate and keen as any of His others.
Align thyself with virtue! Does not America
Extend to all the promises of liberty and justice?
Beset the Legislature with ardor and insistence,
Beseech for all the power of freedom's rights
And privileges. No difference exists between us
In the eyes of God. Hear ye, for mercy's sake!

The Ballad of Doctor James Barry

Margaret Ann Bulkley (c.1789-1865)

On a wet, thunderous night back in fair County Cork,
To an honest green grocer and laboring wife,
With the cord round my neck like a pulsating torque,
I emerged with a howl as a girl into life.

Though my father toiled days at the weigh house as well,
Our money was squandered on liquor and bawds
By my brother. Enticed by the urgings of Hell,
He wagered and lost all we had to the sods.

My father was hauled to the prison for debtors,
Society's dubious cure for all ills. Mother
Begged for relief from our debts and the fetters,
From the artist, Professor James Barry, her brother.

My uncle discharged our debts, and we traveled
To London. His friend, Edward Fryer, taught me.
Thus, chains of benighted detention unraveled.
Enlightened, I thrived, apprehending study.

As a maid, university would be denied.
Dr. Fryer and the General envisaged a plan.
The pseudonymous James Stuart Barry applied,
And Edinburgh accepted, expecting a man.

The General promised that ultimately,
He would take me to Venezuela where
Female doctors were practising openly.
I could be both a doctor and woman there.

In three years, I passed my exams. I studied
Behaviour of men and anatomy both.
Plans for my Venezuelan practice were muddied
By the General's arrest, thereby sullying troth.

My life goal, a doctor, eclipsed my desire
For marriage or raising a child. I decided
The lie must prevail, and my senses conspire
To play the charade with my nature elided.

I continued, an intern, in manly disguise,
Then signed with the Army as surgeon. My post
Was the Cape of Good Hope, where to my great surprise,
I encountered the quandary I dreaded the most.

In spite of my trousers and short-cropped curls,
The governor, Lord Charles Somerset,
Preferred my attentions to obvious girls,
And my natural feminine cravings were whet.

When he learned my true gender, we had an affair
Which we thought we could readily handle.
My mien and our passion did not well compare.
Our deportment created a scandal.

Accusations of homosexuality
Lord Charles and I bravely faced.
In the end, the courts did exonerate me,
But my lover sailed home in disgrace.

He never revealed my secret, and I
Never told him about our child.
I curse and fight duels to fortify
The façade of a man easily riled.

Inspector General of Hospitals now,
Improving hygiene and good health,
I live what society would not allow,
Spurning frailty, beauty, and wealth.

My success as a surgical pioneer
And my sway on the public well-being
Were impossible quite but for means passing queer,
Since full half the world's people need freeing.

Mother of the Regiment

Mary Seacole (1805-1881)

Afro-Caribbean
    My mother was a free woman.

British
    Well-educated by my patroness, I travelled early to London, my second home.

Creole
    Native to neither Africa nor Europe, I am tinged by their mixture.

Doctress
    In this, too, I resemble my mother, skilled in the healing arts.

Eudaemonia
    Action directed by reason effects happiness.

Flamboyant
    Epaulettes, feathers, jewelry, and brightly coloured silks herald one's presence.

Grey-eyed
    My Scotch father was an Army officer whose courage I inherited.

Hotelier
    At Spring Hill, I operated the British Hotel, renowned for our officers' dinner parties.

Improvisator
    Driftwood, iron sheeting, and packing cases sufficed for its building materials.

Jamaica
    The island of my origin is now a British Crown Colony.

Kingston
    I was born in Blundell Hall, my mother's lodging house on East Street near the sea.

Land Transport Corps Hospital
Any succor I can offer, I unstintingly give my sons: the suffering, sick, and wounded.

Myal
Water lily roots, thistle seeds, lemongrass, and other simples.

Nurse
Comforting words, a gentle touch, and tenderness speed healing or soften death.

Obloquy
Bigotry has never vanquished my spirit.

Panama
Dead despite my tears and ministrations, the tiny body gave up cholera's secrets.

Quarter
Those five cold weeks, I brought tea to suffering soldiers awaiting hospital ships.

Royal Surrey Gardens Benefit Festival
England eventually thanked me with the capital needed to pay my creditors.

Sutler
Seacole and Day sold boots, saddlery, tins, cigars, meat, greens, and more.

Theater of Operations
I watched the siege of Sevastopol from the hill where I sold refreshments.

Unguents
My medicine chest, stocked with bandages and powders, is my appendage.

Victorian
Miss Nightingale's nursing services are thoroughly recompensed and lauded.

War
Wherever men lie sick and wounded, it is my privilege to lend assistance.

Xyster

Take pains to scrape out the putrefaction before stitching closed the wound.

Yellow Fever

Calomel, followed by Peruvian bark in brandy, hastens convalescence.

Zest

Life is an adventure from which I never cringe.

Minty

Harriet Tubman (c.1820-1913)

Lord, Your light guides me still,
Walking home with greens to feed
Your blessed veterans. This isn't Egypt,
But it's not Canaan if Negroes can't get
Decent wages for work they did as slaves.

Slaves. My blood boils when I recall the whip,
The screams of my sisters sold down South,
The overseer who broke my skull. Master
Got ready to sell me, but I used everything
Daddy Ben taught me to slip away.

Wading through swamps, up river,
Hiding on islands, sleeping in snatches,
Ear to the ground, I followed the moss
And the drinking gourd north, 'til
You brought me to freedom.

It isn't enough being free
If you can't share that meal
With those that starve, and I did,
Nineteen times. You led me, Lord,
To carry willing family and strangers.

You make me fall down and see
Visions. You speak. I have been
Your scout and spy, Your mouth.
You move the waters of sleep.
Lead us. We'll keep walking.

Nandi Flame

Wangari Maathai (1940-2011)

The women walk to find water
And wood for fire.
They feed the children
And plant the seeds.

Some people say
I am not a good African woman.
I am educated and outspoken.

I protest.
They beat me.
I persist.
They jail me.

But the spirit is fearless,
Like a tree.

As children,
We picked the buds
From the Nandi flame,
Chasing each other,
Laughing, squirting water
From crimson flowers
With yellow-stained hands.

I plant the Nandi flame
For the children,
For Africa,
For joy.

IV.
Glass Scepter

From Concubine to Empress

Wu Zetian (624-705)

In the palace gardens, a serpent
Takes into her body the vermin.

Saved from the rodents' teeth,
Food grows plentiful and verdant.

The palace chambers are clean,
And the kitchens filled with meat.

Well-fed, the people flourish,
And many find enlightenment.

With heavy clubs and sharpened sticks,
Men hunt the serpent in the grass.

Lithe and quick, she blazes paths,
Preserving herself with cunning.

Obstacles must be swept away.
The serpent swallows her daughter.

Empress of expansion, order,
And peace, I am the serpent.

The chronicles of history
Will vindicate my deeds.

North from the Kingdom

Yennenga (12th c.)

I was raised as a warrior and fought beside my father, King Nedega, plunging my spear into the bodies of our enemies, casting my javelin, and sending arrows straight to their mark.

In my thirteenth year, we were ambushed as we hunted elands. My father was wounded, and his horse was killed. I leaped from my stallion and stood astride my father, killing our enemies in all directions with my ebony bow. On our return, the people sang in praise for many days.

The rains came. The wind whispered, Look. See the women nursing their babies, smiling at their children. Hear the women sing to their ancestors of the fruit in their wombs. Feel the earth beating as the women dance, circling the fire, moving their hips like the currents of a great river.

The spear felt heavy in my hands. I want to hear a child laugh, I told my father. He said, You are a warrior, a leader in battle. You will fight, not bear children.

I planted a field of millet. When the crop ripened, I let it rot. This is my life, I told my father. He became angry and locked me away, setting guards to watch.

A horseman came by night and killed the guards. He brought my stallion. I disguised myself as a man, and we escaped. We rode through the land of the Malinké, and there the horseman was killed. I rode north alone.

I crossed a mighty river and entered the forest. A man sat beside his fire. I spoke in a deep voice and greeted him as a man. He invited me to eat and drink. He was handsome and young, dark and strong.

For three days and nights, I listened to his tales of valor and skill hunting elephants. Riale was his name, and my heart longed to beat close to his. For three days, I listened in longing, in love. On the third night, I lifted my helmet, and he knew me as a woman.

Riale and I were married. Our son was born, Ouedraogo, the stallion. He grew to be a great warrior, king of the Mossi.

The wind whispers, Look. You are a woman. A mother.

The Austrian Tribade's Head, Promised to the Sans-Culottes

Marie Antoinette (1755-1793)

His first madness shocked my scalp bald.

Morning smelled of melted silk.
We left in search of fire.
Every exchange—verbal,
Physical, monetary, visual,
Was negotiated by explosions.

We paid for his disintegration
Only with our lives.
We shared our hunger
As tocsins stained the air.

His second madness froze me to my bed.

Noon was black with smoke.
Earthquake weather muttered
Vague obscenities—whose organ
And which finger became
A matter of interpretation.

We built ourselves a second home
Of thistles and tar, giving the earth
Our prayers, our firstborn son,
Our youngest daughter.

His third madness robbed me of my sight.

Evening rustled a parched code.
Predators woke and molted.
The trail of vibrations
Shed by gold and diamonds
Led them to us, and prey fell.

We spoke at the very end of water,
Our ancestors receding in memory.
We offered ourselves in sacrifice
To the swarming six-legged gods.

My Several Natures

Theodora (c.497-548)

It's true, my father was a bear keeper.
My mother was an actress.
(Read "prostitute.")
She carefully lined my eyes and
Dressed me in a ribbon.

I performed at the Hippodrome
As the teaser between chariot races.
Hundreds of thousands of men,
Hooting and throwing coins,
Leered at my Leda impersonation,
Naked on the ground with a goose
Between my thighs, nibbling grain
From my arched body.

I had no choice.
It was that or starve.

Hecebolus kept me 'til bored,
Then beat me and threw me out.

In Antioch, I dreamed of the Demon Lord,
A noble lover, insatiate and smitten.
He carried me to his glittering palace,
Made love to me, and married me.

A prophecy, breathed Macedonia.
I shook my head.
Impossible.

In Constantinople, I lived near the palace.
I spent my days spinning wool and praying.
I found God, and Justinian found me.
He carried me to his glittering palace,
Made love to me, and married me.

He became emperor, and I, his wife,
Became Byzantine Empress, Augusta,
Hailed by hundreds of thousands of men,
Cheering and throwing roses in the Hippodrome
Where I used to lay naked, sprinkled with grain.

Los Toldos

Eva Perón (1919-1952)

Just because people say they like your looks, or the way you sound, doesn't necessarily mean you deserve the attention. It doesn't automatically follow that you have any real talent. Maybe you've just been lucky to show up when the producer was hungry for what you could give him. The director liked the way you smiled because it reminded him of his mother's face on Epiphany.

Yesterday you saw a small brown dog shivering in the street on three legs, and you crossed to the other side for fear it would rub against your white coat. You used to care about suffering. You used to want to do something to help others.

You still dream sometimes. I mean, supposedly we dream all the time, but some dreams you should remember. Last night you dreamed you were in the house where we grew up, the old table where we'd sit to eat and the basin out back where you used to wash the dishes. The plates were all cracked and chipped, and the table was bare. Somehow, you knew the house was empty. When you woke up, you felt terrible, knowing your childhood had been stolen.

Maybe you've finally proved to yourself that you're smart and good. All the headlines and fan letters, people asking you for your autograph, should convince you. But they don't.

Go to bed early tonight and try to wake up feeling strong. Try to dream of accomplishing something worthwhile, something that actually matters.

If you can't learn from your dreams, you're wasting your time.

She Who Is of the Time of Green Corn

Hopokoekau, "Glory of the Morning" (c.1711-c.1832)

In the time of the Earth Digging Moon, I was born at dawn.
In the Thunderbird clan of the Hočąk nation, to the great chief, I was born.

In the end of the Corn Popping Moon, when I was a young *yųgiwi,*
    I became chief.
In the sky at dawn, the Great Star, the warrior god He Who is Girded in
    Blankets aligned with the crescent Moon, goddess who watches women.

In the ranks of the Spirit People who fought our neighbors, the Meskwaki,
    there came a man.
In the time of the Elk Whistling Moon, this man and I were married.

In the seven years we lived together, the Spirit People fought against
    the Meskwaki.
In the eighth year, the war club was put aside, and my husband returned
    to his people.

In the time of his leaving, my two sons remained with me.
In the place of his wife, the chief of her nation, my husband took
    our daughter.

In the years that followed, I led the nation on the warpath against the Illini.
In the wars, we fought the Michigamea and the Cahokia, but with the
    Spirit People we were allied, and my son Čugiga fought the Zaganąš
    with his father.

In the conquest of the Spirit People by the Zaganąš, my husband was killed.
In the time of peace that followed, with the Zaganąš the nation was allied.

In the time of the Deer Antler Shedding Moon, there came an owl.
In the pine forest white with snow, there came an owl that spoke my name.

Oni Pa'a

Queen Liliuokalani (1838-1917)

So now the *haole*
Defy their president—
Steal our islands,
Steal our hearts.
The wind sighs,
Goodbye, goodbye.
With every wave,
I pray *Oli Ho-oikaika*.

What else can I do?
The missionary party
Demands abdication,
Demands annexation.
Haole ships wait
In our harbors.
Haole guns wait
To kill Hawaiians.
So I surrender.
What else can I do?

So I surrender—
With heavy heart
I abdicate—
But *haole* force
Cannot erase
Our dances,
Our chants,
Our songs,
Our drumming,
Our stories,
Our past,
Our future.

Stars of Maui,
Weep, lament
In gentle rain.
Gently stroke
The forest leaves—
Rise like mist
At dawn—
Rise and stand, singing.

The Light of Hope

Benazir Bhutto (1953-2007)

Dirt floor, bare walls.
Sunrays stream
From high windows.
Daughters of the tribes
Bend over desks.
Their pens scratch.
When I come to the door,
They do not look up.
Their shawls spill
Over hunched shoulders—
A snowy mountain,
A cloudless sky,
A grassy hillside,
A rain of crimson petals
In fierce light.

Notes

"Autoretrato Ultimo"

Childhood polio and a near-fatal accident when she was eighteen forced Frida Kahlo to contend with pain, infertility, surgeries, and physical disintegration for the rest of her life. *Autoretrato ultimo* means "last self-portrait," *azul* is "blue," *mi amor* translates to "my love," and *chistes* means "jokes" in Spanish.

"Our Lady of the Chronicles"

Chinese was the official language of men and government in Heian Japan. Murasaki Shikibu, a lady of the court, wrote *The Tale of Genji* in vernacular Japanese. Many consider her novel to be one of the world's first and greatest works of fiction.

"Toward Permanence"

Julia Morgan was the first woman to earn a certificate in architecture from the École des Beaux-Arts in Paris. In 1904, she became the first woman licensed to practice architecture in California. She opened her own firm in San Francisco and designed more than 700 structures in styles ranging from Arts and Crafts to Mediterranean. In 2014, she was posthumously awarded the American Institute of Architects Gold Medal and became the first woman in the AIA College of Fellows.

"Where Sovereign Music Leads"

Renowned as a gifted composer, singer, and instrumentalist in 17th-century Venice, Barbara Strozzi published seven collections of her own vocal music during her lifetime, more than any other musical contemporary.

"Observation"

An English scientist and X-ray crystallographer, Rosalind Franklin published 37 scientific papers on her research into the structures of coal, DNA, and viruses. Her significant contributions to the understanding of DNA included meticulous data and X-ray diffraction images. Questionable behavior within the scientific community and then her death from cancer at age 37 precluded her receiving the 1962 Nobel Prize awarded to her scientific peers Watson, Crick, and Wilson.

"Flyology"

Ada Lovelace collaborated with Charles Babbage on his Analytical Engine, an early mechanical general-purpose computer. She translated an article by the Italian military engineer Luigi Menabrea, and within her copious notes there is an algorithm that she developed that many regard as the first computer program.

"Metamorphosis"

Maria Sibylla Merian funded her own scientific expedition to Surinam. She was 52 years old when she sailed with her daughter from Amsterdam to South America in 1699.

"Viriditas"

When Hildegard von Bingen was seven years old, her parents gave her to the Disibodenberg monastery, where she lived as an anchoress. Elected magistra in 1136, she founded two convents while writing her visionary theology, poetry, music, letters, morality play, and texts on medicine and science. In 2012, Pope Benedict XVI recognized Hildegard as a saint and proclaimed her a Doctor of the Universal Church.

"Singing"

Georgia O'Keeffe was quoted in *The New York Sun* on December 5, 1922, saying: "Singing has always seemed to me the most perfect means of expression. It is so spontaneous. And after singing, I think the violin. Since I cannot sing, I paint."

"Hill Top"

Schooled at home, Beatrix Potter concentrated on natural sciences and art. She illustrated fairy tales and scientific texts and then became famous as the author and illustrator of *The Tale of Peter Rabbit*. She bought Hill Top and took up farming, buying additional farms, parks, and tracts in England's Lake District with the proceeds from her books for children. At her death, she bequeathed 4,300 acres to the National Trust in order to preserve and protect the region's traditional farms and natural scenic beauty.

"Narcisse Noir"

Anaïs Nin continuously kept a journal from age eleven and wrote novels, short stories, erotica, and literary criticism. Expurgated volumes of her diary began to be published in 1966. She lived an extraordinarily free life with many lovers and two husbands simultaneously.

"Red Emma"

During her years in America, Emma Goldman promoted anarchy, worker's rights, sexual freedom, and contraception. She was charged with breaking the Comstock Law, a federal act passed by Congress in 1873 for the "Suppression of Trade in, and Circulation of, Obscene Literature and Articles of Immoral Use." In 1919, she was found guilty of publicly criticizing the United States government and deported to Russia under the Sedition Act of 1918.

"Whaea O, Te Motu"

Whaea O, Te Motu is Māori for "Mother of the Nation," the title given to Dame Whina Cooper in 1957 by the Māori Women's Welfare League, of which she was founding president. *Pākehā* refer to the Europeans who came to her native land, *Aoteraroa*, also called New Zealand. *Tangata whenua* are the indigenous people of New Zealand, literally "people of the land." *Tikanga* are the Māori traditions and customs handed down through time. *Mana* means "authority, prestige, and influence." The *marae* is the traditional Māori meeting place where discussions and formal greetings occur.

"Raised in the Harem"

In 1908, Huda Shaarawi founded the first philanthropic society for Egyptian women. She founded an academic school for girls in 1910 and the Egyptian Feminist Union in 1923.

"Aperture"

Dorothea Lange and other noted photographers were hired to document and publicize the Depression's effects on farmers. Roy Striker, an economist from Columbia University, was put in charge of the "Historical Section" of the Resettlement Administration, an agency that later became the Farm Security Administration. He and his team assembled a collection of more than 80,000 photographs, including Lange's famous "Migrant Mother, Nipomo, California, 1936."

"Culturist"

Madam C. J. Walker was a self-made millionaire, thought by many to be the first woman in America to achieve that status. She organized one of America's first national meetings of businesswomen, the Madam C. J. Walker Hair Culturists Union of America convention, held in Philadelphia in 1917. A generous philanthropist, she was politically and socially active in organizations and causes promoting African American rights and progress.

"La Peregrina"

Born in San Francisco, then a Gold Rush boomtown, Alma Reed became a journalist who evolved into a pioneering archaeological reporter. She was responsible for breaking the story of Chichén Itzá's discovery for *The New York Times*. The song, "La Peregrina," was composed for Alma at the request of Felipe Carrillo Puerto, the Socialist governor of Yucatán who was assassinated by enemy rebels. *Alma* is Spanish for "soul."

"Folk Pornography Exposé"

A journalist, activist, and investigator of lynchings, Ida B. Wells published a brief editorial in her Memphis newspaper, *Free Speech,* suggesting accusations of rape frequently followed the discovery of consensual relationships between black men and white women. Arriving in New York City, she learned that the office of her paper had been burned and her publishing partner run out of town, and crowds of white men were posting themselves outside railway stations in order to lynch her. Knowing black men would be murdered for trying to protect her, she remained in exile for thirty years.

"Pieces of the Mosaic"

In late 1917, Alice Paul was among the women arrested for picketing the White House as "Silent Sentinels" for the cause of women's suffrage. She was sentenced to seven months in jail, held in solitary confinement, denied legal counsel, and, after she began a hunger strike, forcibly fed. Following critical publicity of the prisoners' treatment, President Wilson finally declared his support for women's suffrage. Two years later, the 19th amendment was ratified, granting American women the right to vote in 1920.

"The White Rose"

The White Rose (*die Weiße Rose*) was a non-violent resistance group in Nazi Germany. Members wrote, printed, and distributed pamphlets urging active opposition to the Nazi regime. Sophie Scholl was arrested in February of 1943, found guilty of treason, and executed by guillotine. *Mutti* is a colloquial German word for "mother."

"Barnstorming"

The Dicta Boelcke is a list of maxims for success in aerial combat formulated by the World War I flying ace, Oswald Boelcke. Bessie Coleman was the first African American woman to fly a plane and, in 1921, the first African American to earn an international pilot's license. Her dream of opening an aviation school for African Americans ended with her death at age 34 while practicing for a barnstorming exhibition.

"The Miller's Daughter"

Jane Addams was awarded the Nobel Peace Prize in 1931 for her lifelong work as a pioneering social worker, feminist, pacifist, and internationalist.

"Family 21373"

Oshogatsu is the Japanese celebration of the New Year, and *mochi* is a traditional New Year's food. *Oshogatsu* custom prohibits cleaning the house on the day before New Year, since sweeping away the good spirits will bring bad luck in the coming year. A *daruma* is a Japanese doll without eyes. Customarily, a wish is made and one eye filled in. The doll's other eye is filled in only if the wish comes true. Sox Kitashima and other activists eventually succeeded in securing reparations for the Japanese Americans interned in U.S. concentration camps.

"Hear Ye"

A pioneering African American abolitionist and feminist, Maria W. Stewart's essays and lectures were published in *The Liberator* and in numerous pamphlets. She was the first American-born woman to address a mixed audience of black and white men and women.

"The Ballad of Doctor James Barry"

When Dr. James Barry died in London, the body was buried without a post-mortem. After the funeral, the maid who had laid out the body went public with the information that Dr. Barry was in fact a woman with stretch marks. There was much speculation as to the famous surgeon's actual gender, but the London press published no obituary. The British Army kept Barry's service records sealed for nearly one hundred years. Recently discovered evidence based on handwriting analysis strongly supports the position that Dr. James Barry was a woman from Ireland named Margaret Ann Bulkley.

"Mother of the Regiment"

Mary Seacole published her autobiography *Wonderful Adventures of Mrs. Seacole in Many Lands* in 1857. Eudaemonism is the doctrine that the basis for moral obligations is the tendency of right actions to produce happiness. Myalism, a healing culture brought from Africa, was practiced in 18th- and 19th-century Jamaica by highly skilled women who used plant parts and therapeutic ministrations to effect cures. A xyster is a surgical instrument for scraping bones.

"Minty"

For thirty years after her military service, Harriet Tubman struggled to receive due recompense for her work as a Union spy, nurse, recruiter, and guide. Finally, after the death of her second husband, a Civil War veteran, she was granted a widow's pension of $8 a month. Tubman also worked for women's suffrage and maintained a home in Auburn for the aged and indigent until her death.

"Nandi Flame"

An environmental and political activist in Kenya, Wangari Maathai founded the Green Belt Movement. African women are taught to plant and care for trees, enabling the women to earn money while they restore the environment. Maathai received the Nobel Peace Prize in 2004 "for her contribution to sustainable development, democracy and peace."

"From Concubine to Empress"

Wu Zetian was the only woman to rule as an autonomous female sovereign in Chinese imperial history. Despite accusations of profligate acts and ruthless murders, historians generally credit her with consolidating the Tang dynasty, introducing the meritocratic system for administrative bureaucrats, and expanding China's influence during her fifty years in power.

"North from the Kingdom"

The Mossi people of Burkina Faso regard Yennenga as the mother of their kingdom. Her son, Ouedraogo, was the first in a chain of thirty monarchs, an unbroken dynasty extending from the 12th century to the present.

"The Austrian Tribade's Head, Promised to the Sans-Culottes"

Marie Antoinette was the fifteenth child of Francis I, Holy Roman Emperor, and Empress Maria Theresa. They arranged Marie Antoinette's marriage to the Dauphin of France, and she became Queen of France and Navarre when her husband ascended the throne as Louis XVI. *Tribade* was an 18th-century French slur meaning "lesbian," and the *sans-culottes*, literally "without trousers," were the working class and poor of France. Marie Antoinette suffered scurrilous libel and vitriolic contempt during her husband's reign, in large part because she was Austrian.

"My Several Natures"

As Byzantine empress, Theodora exerted a powerful influence on her husband, Emperor Justinian I. During the Nika uprising, her courageous speech to the government council convinced Justinian and his generals to attack the rebellious faction rather than flee for their lives. Theodora was instrumental in the passage of laws promoting greater economic autonomy for women and providing legal protection for widows, divorcees, prostitutes, and children.

"Los Toldos"

Eva Perón was born in Los Toldos, a small village in Buenos Aires province. She dropped out of high school to become an actress and radio star in the capital city. After her marriage to Colonel Juan Perón, elected president of Argentina in 1946, Evita worked on behalf of Argentinian women and children, labor, and the welfare of the *descamisados*, Argentina's working class and poor, until her death.

"She Who Is of the Time of Green Corn"

Hopokoekau was the chief of the Thunderbird clan of the Hočąk nation, or Winnebago, who lived in a large village on Doty Island in present-day Wisconsin. *Yugiwi* means "leader-woman." The Spirit People were the French.

"Oni Pa'a"

Oni pa'a is Hawaiian for "persevere" or "stand firm." *Haole* are the non-Hawaiians who came to the islands of Hawaii. Liliuokalani was the last Hawaiian monarch. In 1893, haole business interests and annexationists abrogated Queen Liliuokalani's authority, defied President Cleveland's order that she be restored as monarch, and forced her abdication. *Oli Ho-oikaika,* "Prayer for Strength," is an anonymous Hawaiian poem.

"The Light of Hope"

Following the execution of her father, former Prime Minister Zulfikar Ali Bhutto, Benazir Bhutto spent many years under house arrest, imprisoned, and in exile. Leader of the Pakistan People's Party, she became Prime Minister of Pakistan in 1988 and served two non-consecutive terms. Benazir Bhutto was the first woman to head a modern Muslim nation. She was assassinated in 2007.

Sources

Frida Kahlo

Herrera, Hayden. *Frida: A Biography of Frida Kahlo.* New York: HarperCollins, 1983.

Herrera, Hayden. *Frida Kahlo: The Paintings.* New York: HarperCollins, 1991.

Kahlo, Frida. *The Diary of Frida Kahlo: An Intimate Self-Portrait.* Translated by Barbara Crow de Toledo and Ricardo Pohlenz. New York: Abrams, 1995.

Murasaki Shikibu

Ikeda, Daisaku. *On the Japanese Classics.* Translated by Burton Watson, 95-152. New York: Weatherhill, 1979.

Murasaki Shikibu. *The Tale of Genji.* Translated by Arthur Waley. New York: Modern Library, 1960.

Tyler, Royall. "Murasaki Shikibu: Brief Life of a Legendary Novelist." *Harvard Magazine,* May-June 2002: 32-33.

Julia Morgan

Boutelle, Sara Holmes. *Julia Morgan, Architect.* New York: Abbeville Press, 1988.

Mortice, Zach. "Julia Morgan, FAIA—2014 AIA Gold Medal Recipient." *American Institute of Architects* 20, December 13, 2013.

Barbara Strozzi

Beer, Anna. "Strozzi." In *Sounds and Sweet Airs: The Forgotten Women of Classical Music,* 53-87. London: Oneworld Publications, 2016.

Stevenson, Joseph. "Barbara Strozzi." *AllMusic,* 2016.

Rosalind Franklin

Holt, Jim. "Photo Finish." *New Yorker,* October 28, 2002.

Maddox, Brenda. *Rosalind Franklin: The Dark Lady of DNA.* London: HarperCollins, 2002.

Ada Lovelace

Essinger, James. *Ada's Algorithm: How Lord Byron's Daughter Ada Lovelace Launched the Digital Age.* Brooklyn: Melville House, 2015.

Morais, Betsy. "Ada Lovelace, the First Tech Visionary." *New Yorker,* October 15, 2013.

Maria Sibylla Merian

Davis, Natalie Zemon. "Metamorphoses: Maria Sibylla Merian." In *Women on the Margins: Three Seventeenth-Century Lives,* 140-202. Cambridge: Harvard University Press, 1995.

Duennes, Michelle. "Famous Female Entomologists Part 4: Maria Sibylla Merian, the Mother of Entomology." *Entomology Today,* February 26, 2015.

Etheridge, Kay. "Maria Sibylla Merian: The First Ecologist?" In *Women and Science: Figures and Representations—17th Century to Present,* edited by V. Molinari and D. Andreolle, 31-49. Cambridge Scholars Publishing, 2011.

Todd, Kim. *Chrysalis: Maria Sibylla Merian and the Secrets of Metamorphosis.* Orlando: Harcourt, 2007.

Hildegard von Bingen

Flanagan, Sabina. *Hildegard of Bingen, 1098-1179: A Visionary Life.* New York: Routledge, 1998.

McGuire, K.C. *International Society of Hildegard von Bingen Studies.* July 14, 2014.

Vision—Aus dem Leben der Hildegard von Bingen. Directed by Margarethe von Trotta, *Zeitgeist,* 2009.

Georgia O'Keeffe

Castro, Jan Garden. *The Art & Life of Georgia O'Keeffe.* New York: Crown Publishers, 1985.

Turner, Elizabeth Hutton. "I Can't Sing So I Paint." In *Georgia O'Keeffe & Alfred Stieglitz: Two Lives,* edited by Alexandra Arrowsmith and Thomas West, 79-86. New York: HarperCollins, 1992.

Beatrix Potter

Foote, Timothy. "A Tale of Some Tales, and the Story of Their Shy Creator." *Smithsonian Magazine* 19 no. 10: 80-91, January 1989.

Hobbs, Anne Stevenson. *Beatrix Potter's Art.* Middlesex: Frederick Warne, 1989.

Lear, Linda. *Beatrix Potter: A Life in Nature.* New York: St. Martin's Griffin, 2007.

Anaïs Nin

Bair, Deirdre. *Anais Nin: A Biography.* New York: G. P. Putnam's Sons, 1995.

Nin, Anaïs. *Henry and June.* San Diego: Harcourt Brace Jovanovich, 1986.

Nin, Anaïs. *The Diary of Anaïs Nin,* Vols. 1-5. New York: Mariner Books, 1969-1975.

Emma Goldman

Goldman, Emma. *Living My Life.* New York: Penguin Books, 2006.

Whina Te Wake Cooper

Barber, David. "Obituary: Dame Whina Cooper." *Independent,* March 27, 1994.

King, Michael. "Cooper, Whina." *Te Ara—The Encyclopedia of New Zealand,* June 6, 2013.

Taylor, Melvin. "Whina Cooper." *Te Ao Hou* 12: 17-19, September 1955. *National Library of New Zealand.*

Huda Shaarawi

Quawas, Rula B. "A Sea Captain in Her Own Right: Navigating the Feminist Thought of Huda Shaarawi." *Journal of International Women's Studies* 8, no.1: 219-235, 2006.

Shaarawi, Huda. *Harem Years: The Memoirs of an Egyptian Feminist.* New York: The Feminist Press, 1986.

Dorothea Lange

Doud, Richard. "Oral History Interview with Dorothea Lange, 1964 May 22." *Archives of American Art, Smithsonian Institution.*

Meltzer, Milton. *Dorothea Lange: A Photographer's Life.* New York: Farrar Straus Giroux, 1978.

Madam C. J. Walker

Bundles, A'Lelia. *On Her Own Ground: The Life and Times of Madam C. J. Walker.* New York: Scribner, 2001.

Alma Reed

May, Antoinette. *Passionate Pilgrim: The Extraordinary Life of Alma Reed.* New York: Paragon House, 1993.

Reed, Alma. *Peregrina: Love and Death in Mexico.* University of Texas Press, 2007.

Ida B. Wells

Giddings, Paula J. *Ida: A Sword Among Lions*. New York: HarperCollins, 2008.

Alice Paul

Iron Jawed Angels. Directed by Katja von Garnier, HBO Films, 2004.

Zahniser, J.D. and Amelia R. Fry. *Alice Paul: Claiming Power*. New York: Oxford University Press, 2014.

Sophie Scholl

Dumbach, Annette and Jud Newborn. *Sophie Scholl and the White Rose*. Oxford: Oneworld, 2007.

Scholl, Inge. *The White Rose: Munich, 1942-1943*. Middletown: Wesleyan, 1983.

Sophie Scholl—Die letzen Tage. Directed by Marc Rothemund, X Verleih AG, 2005.

Bessie Coleman

Rich, Doris L. *Queen Bess: Daredevil Aviator*. Washington, DC: Smithsonian Institution Press, 1993.

Spivey, Lynn. "Bessie Coleman." Atlanta Historical Museum, 2008.

Jane Addams

Addams, Jane. *The Spirit of Youth and the City Streets*. Macmillan, 1909.

Linn, James Weber. *Jane Addams*. New York: D. Appleton-Century, 1935.

Tsuyako "Sox" Kitashima

Kitashima, Tsuyako and Joy K. Morimoto. *Birth of an Activist: The Sox Kitashima Story*. San Mateo: Asian American Curriculum Project, 2003.

Maria W. Stewart

Stewart, Maria W. *Maria W. Stewart, America's First Black Woman Political Writer: Essays and Speeches*. Edited by Marilyn Richardson. Bloomington: Indiana University Press, 1987.

Margaret Ann Bulkley

Hume, Robert. "The Anatomy of a Lie—The Irish Woman Who Lived As a Man to Practice Medicine." *Irish Examiner*, August 1, 2014.

"Margaret Ann Bulkley: The Extraordinary Doctor James Barry." *A Silver Voice From Ireland*, July 17, 2011.

Pain, Stephanie. "Histories: The 'Male' Military Surgeon Who Wasn't." *New Scientist* 2646, March 5, 2008.

Mary Seacole

Robinson, Jane. *Mary Seacole: The Most Famous Black Woman of the Victorian Age.* New York: Carroll & Graf Publishers, 2004.

Seacole, Mary. *Wonderful Adventures of Mrs. Seacole in Many Lands.* London: Penguin Classics, 2005.

Harriet Tubman

Clinton, Catherine. *Harriet Tubman: The Road to Freedom.* New York: Back Bay Books, 2005.

Wangari Maathai

Gilson, Dave. "'I Will Disappear Into the Forest': An Interview With Wangari Maathai." *Mother Jones,* January 5, 2005.

MacDonald, Mia. "The Green Belt Movement: The Story of Wangari Maathai." *Yes Magazine,* March 25, 2005.

Shapiro, Leo. "Spathodea campanulata." *Encyclopedia of Life,* 2016.

"Wangari Maathai." *The Green Belt Movement,* 2016.

"Wangari Maathai—Biographical." *Nobelprize.org,* 2014.

Wu Zetien

Clements, Jonathan. *Wu: The Chinese Empress Who Schemed, Seduced, and Murdered Her Way Her Way to Become a Living God.* USA: Albert Bridge Books, 2014.

Dash, Mike. "The Demonization of Empress Wu." *Smithsonian,* August 10, 2012.

Paul, Diana. "Empress Wu and the Historians: A Tyrant and Saint of Classical China." In *Unspoken Worlds: Women's Religious Lives in Non-Western Cultures,* edited by Nancy A. Falk and Rita M. Gross, 191-206. San Francisco: Harper & Row, 1980.

Yennenga

Carter, Cynthia Jacobs. *Africana Woman: Her Story Through Time,* 28-31. Washington, DC: National Geographic, 2003.

Schwarz-Bart, Simone and Andre. *In Praise of Black Women, Volume 1: Ancient African Queens.* Translated by Rose-Myriam Réjouis and Val Vinokurov, 100-115. Madison: University of Wisconsin Press, 2001.

Marie Antoinette

Fraser, Antonia. *Marie Antoinette: The Journey.* New York: Doubleday, 2001.

Theodora

Cesaretti, Paolo. *Theodora: Empress of Byzantium.* Translated by Rosanna M. Giammanco Frongia. New York: Magowan Publishing, 2004.

Eva Perón

Fraser, Nicholas and Marysa Navarro. *Evita: The Real Life of Eva Perón.* New York: W.W. Norton, 1996.

Hopokoekau, "Glory of the Morning"

Dieterle, Richard L. "The Glory of the Morning." *Encyclopedia of Hočąk (Winnebago) Mythology,* 2005.

McBride, Genevieve G. "Women's Wisconsin: From Native Matriarchies to the New Millenium." *Wisconsin Magazine of History* 89, no.2: 12-15, Winter 2005-2006.

Quaife, Milo Milton. "Stories of Wisconsin: Glory of the Morning." *Milwaukee Journal,* August 15, 1925.

Queen Liliuokalani

Allen, Helena G. *The Betrayal of Liliuokalani: Last Queen of Hawaii 1838-1917.* Honolulu: Mutual Publishing, 1991.

"Oli Ho-oikaika/Prayer for Strength." *Poetry Chaikhana,* 2015.

Benazir Bhutto

Bhutto, Benazir. *Daughter of Destiny.* New York: Harper Perennial, 2007.

Weaver, Mary Anne. "Bhutto's Fateful Moment." *New Yorker,* October 4, 1993.

Acknowledgments

Grateful acknowledgment is given to the following publications in which some of these poems first appeared:

Describing the Depths: "Nandi Flame"
Homestead Review: "Viriditas," "Raised in the Harem," "Minty," "She Who Is of the Time of Green Corn"
Lone Star Legacy: "Barnstorming"
Santa Fe Literary Review: "Our Lady of the Chronicles"
Steam Ticket: "Red Emma"

Special thanks to Bradley Michael Rodgers, whose musical composition graced the poem, "Where Sovereign Music Leads," first performed on May 17, 2016, at the California State University Stanislaus 31st Annual Student Composition and New Music Festival.

Cover photo, "Forest, Light, Autumn, Trees," by Gewa; author photo by Ashley Rose Tacheira; cover and interior book design by Diane Kistner; Chaparral Pro text and titling

About FutureCycle Press

FutureCycle Press is dedicated to publishing lasting English-language poetry books, chapbooks, and anthologies in both print-on-demand and Kindle ebook formats. Founded in 2007 by long-time independent editor/publishers and partners Diane Kistner and Robert S. King, the press incorporated as a nonprofit in 2012. A number of our editors are distinguished poets and writers in their own right, and we have been actively involved in the small press movement going back to the early seventies.

The FutureCycle Poetry Book Prize and honorarium is awarded annually for the best full-length volume of poetry we publish in a calendar year. Intro-duced in 2013, our Good Works projects are anthologies devoted to issues of universal significance, with all proceeds donated to a related worthy cause. Our Selected Poems series highlights contemporary poets with a substantial body of work to their credit; with this series we strive to resurrect work that has had limited distribution and is now out of print.

We are dedicated to giving all of the authors we publish the care their work deserves, making our catalog of titles the most diverse and distinguished it can be, and paying forward any earnings to fund more great books.

We've learned a few things about independent publishing over the years. We've also evolved a unique, resilient publishing model that allows us to focus mainly on vetting and preserving for posterity poetry collections of excep-tional quality without becoming overwhelmed with bookkeeping and mailing, fundraising activities, or taxing editorial and production "bubbles." To learn more about what we are doing, come see us at www.futurecycle.org.

The FutureCycle Poetry Book Prize

All full-length volumes of poetry published by FutureCycle Press in a given calendar year are considered for the annual FutureCycle Poetry Book Prize. This allows us to consider each submission on its own merits, outside of the context of a contest. Too, the judges see the finished book, which will have benefitted from the beautiful book design and strong editorial gloss we are famous for.

The book ranked the best in judging is announced as the prize-winner in the subsequent year. There is no fixed monetary award; instead, the winning poet receives an honorarium of 20% of the total net royalties from all poetry books and chapbooks the press sold online in the year the winning book was published. The winner is also accorded the honor of being on the panel of judges for the next year's competition; all judges receive copies of all contending books to keep for their personal library.